101 Coolest Things to Do

in Thailand

Introduction

So you're going to Thailand, huh? You lucky lucky thing! You are sure in for a treat because Thailand is truly one of the most magical countries on this planet. There's a mix of ancient temples, incredible street food, and amazing nightlife and shopping that makes Thailand one of the most enduringly popular tourist destinations on the planet.

In this guide, we'll be giving you the low down on:
- the very best things to shove in your pie hole, from street food staples to gourmet restaurants
- incredible adventure activities, from rafting in bat caves to abseiling down cascading waterfalls
- the best shopping so that you can take a little piece of Thailand back home with you
- the most unusual accommodation choices like staying in a jungle treehouse or on a floating boat in a mangrove forest
- the coolest historical and cultural sights that you simply cannot afford to miss
- where to party like a Thai person and make local friends
- and tonnes more coolness besides!

Let's not waste any more time – here are the 101 coolest things not to miss in Thailand!

1. Put Lots of Papaya Salad Into Your Mouth

If there is one place on earth where you have to try all of the street food available to you, it's Thailand. One of the staple dishes that you'll find in absolutely every region of the country is papaya salad. Beautifully fresh green papaya is chopped up with tomato, snake beans, dried shrimp, and very often, an extraordinarily spicy dressing. In Thai, the dish is called "Som Tum" so look out for it on street corners.

2. Learn Circus Tricks at Pai Circus School

Pai is the hippie epicentre of Thailand, and so it should come as no surprise that this small Thai town in the northern hills is home to a circus school. This is a place where backpackers can go, completely free of charge, and learn skills such as juggling and fire dancing. If you get really into it, you might want to consider sticking around for a longer period of time and staying on their property because they also have rooms available.

3. Eat Seafood at a Floating Market

When in Thailand, and particularly Bangkok, you simply have to visit a floating market. There are many to choose from, and it's important to choose the right one, otherwise you'll be surrounded by tourists and charged exorbitant prices. The place to go is Khlong Lat Mayom Floating Market. This is very "off the beaten track" and gives you a real sense of authentic floating market culture, when all local Thai people bought their groceries on floating riverboats. And the thing to eat here is seafood. You will find gigantic crabs, enormous river prawns, and all kinds of delicacies in between.

4. Take a Ride on the Death Railway in Kanchanaburi

Given its name, you may want to give this train a miss, but pinkie promise, you *probably* won't die. Actually, this is an incredibly scenic two hour journey that takes you from Kanchanaburi to Nam Tok. This train is actually called the Death Railway because a huge number of prisoners of war died during its construction (the Japanese had this built as a route from Thailand to Burma during WWII) – nobody has actually died on its journey, so feel free to enjoy the view!

5. Test Your Food Limits with Durian

All across Thailand, there is one particular fruit that the locals love to eat, but that often doesn't sit quite so well with tourists, and that's durian, otherwise known as The Stinky Fruit. Yup, it stinks. If you ever walk on a Thai street and it suddenly smells like you're on a garbage heap, the culprit could well be this local delicacy. The good news is the taste is not quite as offensive as the smell, and many people can't get enough of the fruit once they are accustomed to it. Its flesh is creamy and custardy, and you can find it all around the country.

6. Chew the Fat With Buddhist Monks

Visiting Thailand provides an extraordinary opportunity to learn all about Buddhist religion and culture. Of course, there are many temples that you can visit, but a sure-fire way to advance your learning is by taking part in a Monk Chat at Wat Chedi Luang in Chiang Mai. At this temple, there are set times when the monks invite you into the temple, and you can ask them any questions that you want, from their daily lifestyle to what they eat, to what made them become a monk in the first place.

7. Go Whale Watching in Petchaburi

Okay, so whale watching isn't exactly an activity that you associate with Thailand, but in fact, there are whales to be spotted in the Gulf of Thailand, which is only a two hour drive from Bangkok, making whale watching an ideal day trip and escape from the city. A tour company called Hivesters organises boat tours out on to the water, and you'll enjoy your time on a simple Thai fishing boat while being able to spot beautiful whales coming up for air in the water.

8. Eat an Isaan Sausage or Five

Sausages are a big deal right across Thailand, but each region has its own particular variety. One that really stands out is the Isaan sausage (and it's a good enough to visit the region alone) because this sausage is actually fermented, giving it a really unique sour taste. There is also fermented sticky rice right there inside the sausage, and because people from Isaan love a little bit of spice, it's often served alongside sliced chilli and ginger.

9. Get Tatted Up at Sak Yant Tattoo Festival

Back home, tattoos might be something that you choose to have on your body because it looks pretty, but at this festival, all the tattoos are created by trained monks, and the tattoos are supposed to provide both spiritual and physical protection. Even Angelina Jolie has had a tattoo from one of these monks, and if it's good enough for Angie, it's good enough for us. When you're at the festival, you'll see the people getting tattooed going into a trance and enacting the animals that are tattooed on to their bodies. The festival takes place in Nakhon Chai each February.

10. Have a Gay Ol' Time on Silom Soi 4

Thailand is a spectacularly gay country, and Bangkok is the epicentre of all of that gayness. If you are gay, or even if you aren't and just want to have a fun night out, the place to party is the Silom neighbourhood in the centre of Bangkok, and Silom Soi 4 is the street with the largest concentration of gay bars. Telephone Bar and Balcony Bar are the two nightlife stalwarts that have been around for decades. There is open air seating, a fun crowd, karaoke, and cheap drinks on every night of the week.

11. Bathe With Elephants at Elephant Nature Park

Elephants are beautiful creatures and that's exactly why you should never ride them. They are generally kept in poor conditions, but the Elephant Nature Park in Chiang Mai is an exception. At this park, all the elephants are rescued and rehabilitated. You'll learn about the impact of travel and tourism on elephants and how to look after them in a caring way. Plus, you'll be able to share a river bath with the elephants too!

12. Enjoy a Night Out on Khao San Road

Khao San Road is a love it or hate it kind of place, but it's important to experience it for one night. Khao San Road is the main backpacker street in Bangkok where you can find ridiculously cheap plates of pad thai, beer that flows endlessly, and lots of fun to be had. This is not exactly the place to experience an authentic taste of Thailand, but if you want to meet people and you want to dance until dawn, it honestly can't be beaten.

13. Enjoy a Massage… in a Women's Prison!

Thailand is the best country on earth for incredible massages at a rock bottom prices. In some places, you might even be able to find a massage for $3 per hour. And for a one of a kind massage experience head straight to the Chiang Mai Correctional Women's Institution where inmates from a local prison give tourists massages. These are all women who committed petty crimes, and are given this training so that they have a skill when they leave the facility. They benefit, you benefit.

14. Let Loose at a Full Moon Party

One of the major reasons that backpackers choose to visit Thailand in the first place is the epic full moon parties that take place on a few of the islands, most famously Ko Phangan and Ko Phi Phi. These happen the night before or after every full moon, when the sky is illuminated beautifully, and hordes of backpackers descend on the beach and party until the sun comes up. It's not for everyone, but if you're a party person, you won't want to miss it.

15. Visit Mikkeller for a Truly Awesome Beer

Beer is most definitely "a thing" in Thailand. You'll be able to spot the usual Chang and Singha brands all over the place, and these beers do the job, but if you really want to try something special, you need to find your way to Mikkeller in the Ekkemai district of Bangkok. They serve international and local craft beers for you to drink, and some delectable food options such as fries with truffle oil and a fried egg.

16. Get Physical With Muay Thai Boxing in Phuket

Want to learn a Thai martial art while you're on your trip to Thailand? The island of Phuket is the place to go with numerous Thai boxing camps. Muay Thai is a particularly tough sport because it involves vigorous use of all of your limbs, including fists, elbows, knees and shins. Tiger Muay Thai & Mixed Martial Arts Camp is probably the best known and loved camp on the island, covering 2 acres of land and receiving up to 400 trainees each and every month.

17. Get Lost at Chatutchak Weekend Market

Market culture is super important in Thailand, and the local population love to spend their days shopping, whether it's for streetside snacks or quirky fashion. The biggest outdoor market in Bangkok is the Chatuchak Weekend Market, and to say it's huge is an understatement. You will get lost, there is no way around it, and that's half of the adventure. Inside the market you can buy vintage fashion at rock bottom prices, homewares, candles, plants, tonnes of food, and just about everything in between. Visit from Friday to Sunday.

18. Be Captivated by the Extraordinary Mae Fah Luang Garden

If you happen to be in the north of Thailand, drive one hour north of Chiang Rai and you will find yourself at the magical Mae Fah Lung Garden, beautifully landscaped gardens that sit atop the Doi Tung mountain. The gardens were started by the present Thai King's late mother who wanted to offer local people the kind of temperate garden they would find abroad. And because the gardens are official royal property, you should dress modestly when you visit!

19. Learn about Thailand's Silk Trade in Bangkok

Jim Thompson was the American who saw an opportunity for big business with Thai Silk and transformed it into a global industry. In Bangkok, you can visit his extraordinarily beautiful Thai teak house and gardens, learn about the man, learn about the silk trade, and spend time in a beautiful oasis is the centre of Thailand's capital.

20. Visit a Thai Coffee Plantation in the Thai Hills

Want to get away from the hustle and bustle of Bangkok? The cool hills of the north are the perfect place to do so, and it's there that you can experience a trip to the Doi Chang coffee plantation, and learn exactly how some of the finest coffee in the world is produced. The views are beyond incredible, and of course, the coffee plantation also has its own coffeehouse where you can sip on some of the good stuff. Bags of fresh coffee beans from the plantation also make perfect gifts for friends and family back home.

21. Understand Ancient Thai History at Ayutthaya

Before Thailand was called Thailand, a breadth of land across southeast Asia was called Siam, and the capital of Siam was called Ayutthaya, just one hour south of Bangkok today. This was the capital of Siam from the mid 14th century until the Burmese overran it in the late 18th century. Ayutthaya was truly magnificent, set on a Riverine Island, and the seat of power and trade throughout many centuries. You can visit today to discover ancient temples, the history of trade in Siam, and many ruins from centuries past.

22. Visit the While Temple in Chiang Rai

When travellers visit the north of Thailand, they often stick to Chiang Mai and ignore some of the surrounding gems. But you should absolutely make the effort to stay in Chiang Rai for a couple of nights, if for nothing more than to experience all the majesty of the incredible White Temple, also known as Wat Rong Khun. It is uncommon to see a temple all in white in Thailand, and the effect is truly breath taking. What's more, entrance to the impressive complex is totally free.

23. Enjoy the Sunday Walking Market in Chiang Mai

Each and every Sunday, the centre of Chiang Mai city in northern Thailand totally transforms with an open air walking market. This market that winds through the streets offers a great opportunity to do some cheap shopping, eat some local food, and even have a foot massage on the street.

24. Visit a Hollywood Movie Set

Did you see that movie, The Beach? Of course you did! Well, the place where Leonardo di Caprio jumps off the boat and declares "I found it!" is an isolated beach called Maya Bay on Koh Phi Phi Leh. Of course, thanks to the movie, this beach is no longer quite the unspoiled beach paradise that it once was, but it's still certainly worth a visit, if only to say that you've stepped on the same sand as Leo.

25. Find the Perfect Beach on Ko Phangan

Ko Phangan is one of the better known Thai islands, and as a result, there are a lot of tourists there. This isn't necessarily a bad thing. If you like to party, it's the place to be. Some people don't realise, however, that there is a different side to the island – literally. Most tourists stick to the south, but there is a whole other world on the north side. Bottle Beach is one of the most spectacular beaches you will ever visit, and because it can only be accessed by boat, you can pretty much guarantee that it's not going to be swarming with tourists and partygoers.

26. Explore Burmese Culture in Mae Hong Son

Unless they are actually crossing the border to get into Myanmar, many travellers don't find their way so far north and to the small town of Mae Hong Son, a town that sits right on the border, and thus has huge influences from neighbouring Burma. There is a beautiful lake set right in the centre of the town, there are Shan style temples located around the hilly countryside, and there is plenty of Burmese style food to chow down on.

27. Explore Local Living by Couchsurfing in a Thai Home

Staying in hostels can be a lot of fun. You can meet other travellers and drinking buddies, but it doesn't exactly help you to connect with local people. If this is a priority for you, consider Couchsurfing.com. Create your Couchsurfing profile and you can connect with local people all over the country, who will invite you into their homes to stay on their couch for free. The idea of the free accommodation is not just to have a place to crash, but to have a genuine cultural exchange so you can learn more about Thailand and Thai people.

28. Celebrate Yi Peng Festival in Chiang Mai

When in Thailand, it's a really fantastic idea to get under the skin of Thai culture by celebrating some of the local festivities alongside the locals. In Chiang Mai in the north of Thailand, there is a lights festival called Yi Peng, a festival that pays respect to the Buddha. During this festival, lights are lit within lanterns, which are then released into the air. You can see hundreds of small lights lighting up the black sky at the same time, and the view is absolutely incredible. The exact date changes each year, but the festival usually takes place in mid to late November.

29. Visit the Ancient Lost City, Wiang Kum Kam

Just over 30 years ago, ancient tablets were found underneath a temple, just 5km southeast of Chiang Mai city. This led to the discovery of a complete ancient city called Wiang Kum Kam that dates right back to the eighth century. The whole site has been excavated and you can now visit Wiang Kum Kam, but it's pretty much impossible to do so on foot because it's so large. Instead, opt for one of the local guides who can show you around via pony carriage.

30. See the Famous Reclining Buddha at Wat Pho

Wat Pho is simply one of the most impressive Buddhist temple complexes in the world, dating back to the 16th century. One of the most breath taking temples within the complex is the Temple of the Reclining Buddha. The reclining Buddha is 46 metres long, and its sheer scale is incredible. A must visit on a trip to Thailand's capital.

31. Celebrate the Festival of Ghosts in Dan Sai

The town of Dan Sai is remote and very much not on the tourist trail. That's reason enough for adventurous travellers to explore Dan Sai, but their festival of ghosts or Phi Ta Khon really puts the icing on the cake. Young men wear colourful masks and ghoulish costumes to embody fearsome ghosts around the temple in the centre of town. The dates of the festival change every year but it typically takes place in early July.

32. Sit in Silence for Ten Days

If you want to get to grips with Thai culture, it's really important to take the time to understand Buddhism and meditation. Of course, you can read up on these subjects, but you can take your understanding to a deeper level by actually experiencing an intensive meditation retreat with monks in a temple. The Wat Suan Mokh temple in the south is probably the most famous of these temples offering retreats, and don't expect any luxury – you'll be in complete silence for 10 days and sleeping on a concrete bed. But it might just change your life.

33. Explore the Ancient Ruins of Buriram

Buriram is a little explored city in the Isaan region of Thailand but it's well worth a visit if you want to learn more about Thai history because the place is full of sandstone sculptures from its Khmer heritage. There is a historical park reachable from the city centre, and the locals are extremely welcoming to the few foreigners who make their way to Buriram.

34. Eat Until You're Stuffed at a Bangkok Food Court

Bangkok street food is truly an awesome thing, but the Bangkok humidity, well, not so much. That's when it's time to retire to the air conditioned interiors of one of Bangkok's many food courts. Nearly all the malls across the city will have its own food court, but these are not created equally. For the best and the cheapest fare, waste no time in heading straight to Terminal 21 in the Sukhumvit area. There is so much variety, the quality is excellent across the board, and it's a great place to try a lot of cheap dishes all in one space.

35. Celebrate Songkran….Wherever You Happen to Be!

Songkran is the celebration of Thai New Year, and while the dates change every year, this festival is generally celebrated in April. This festival is such a big deal that it really doesn't matter where you are in Thailand to celebrate – you'll have a great time regardless. During Songkran, it's customary to tip water over everyone in the street. Streets will be full of buckets, water guns, and water bombs, and believe us when we say it's a whole lot of fun – just remember to pack your waterproofs.

36. Take a Boat Ride in Bangkok

Bangkok maybe bustling, but things get a little more peaceful along the river that cuts the city straight in half. The river isn't just something pretty to look at, but you can actually ride up and down the river on public transport. It's a wonderful way to see the city, and for a fraction of the cost of a structured tour.

37. Treat Yourself to Crunchy Oyster Omelettes in Bangkok

You might be wondering what is so special about an omelette, but you clearly haven't tucked into one of the delicious crunchy oyster omelettes at Nai Mong Hoy Tod, a tiny eatery in Bangkok's Chinatown. The omelettes are jam packed with juicy oysters, and the omelette is fried so it's golden and crunchy on the outside but still soft and succulent when you get to the centre. A true Bangkok treat that you cannot miss.

38. Stroll along Pai's Walking Street

If you're into hippies or you are one yourself, Pai is absolutely the town in Thailand for you. And practically every evening, the tourist hippie population comes together on the walking street. Of course, you can buy all the standard but delicious Thai eats as well as lots of international fare, you can spend all of your money on those floaty hippie pants, and make yourself some hippie friends.

39. Shop Until You Drop at Asiatique

If you love shopping, there is no doubt that you will love Bangkok, but the sheer expanse of the city and all the different malls and markets can be overwhelming to say the least. The solution is Asiatique, a cute spot along the river that now plays host to 1500 incredible boutiques. At night, there are innumerable restaurants where you can eat, and there is even the Big Wheel of Bangkok, from which you'll have an incredible view of the whole city.

40. Play With Cats While You Eat Dessert... of Course

The cat café trend is officially everywhere, including the most trendy neighbourhood of Bangkok - Sukhumvit. At Cataholic Café, you will be asked to sanitise your hands before you enter, and then you will have the opportunity to play with adorable kitties while you treat yourself to any number of delicious Thai desserts and coffees on the menu.

41. Tour the Chalong Bay Rum Distillery

When people visit the island of Phuket, they tend to spend their days lazing on the beach and their evenings partying until the sun comes up. But if you want to add something a little different to your stay in Phuket, it's a great idea to take a tour of the only rum distillery on the island. You'll learn all about rum production, you can learn how to make delicious rum cocktails, and of course you can sample one or two as well.

42. Devour a Traditional Thai Breakfast in Bangkok

There are endless culinary options in Bangkok, and one of the most special of them all is a café called On Lok Yun in the Chinatown area of Bangkok. This place has a simple toast menu with just five items, and the thing to opt for is the traditional custard toast. The fluffy bread against the silky custard is honestly a dream come true. There is strong, sweet coffee too, and lots of stares because you're likely to be the only non-Thai person under 50 years old in the place!

43. Be Wowed by Phuket's Big Buddha

If you stay in the southern part of Phuket Island, you are bound to notice a huge Buddha figure that looms over the skyline. The 45 metre Buddha made from Burmese marble sits on top of a hill, which makes for an epic morning hike. Once you are at the top of the hill, not only can you get up and close with the impressive Buddha figure but you'll have a ridiculously amazing view of all of Phuket island. And you will have gotten your exercise for the day – bonus.

44. Discover Island Paradise on Ko Mak

There are so many paradise islands in Thailand and each one has its own culture and feel. Of course, most people have heard of the major islands like Phuket and Ko Phangan but what if you want to find unspoiled paradise, with fine sand, clear waters, and relatively few tourists? In that case, waste no time and head straight to Ko Mak in the Trat region of Thailand. This place is sleepy, beautiful, you'll be lucky to find internet, and there are no ATMs on the island – perfect for a relaxing and magical getaway.

45. Trek around Chiang Mai

Once you make it to the north of Thailand, the views, the culture, the food, and everything in between is totally different from the south. Up in the north, around Chiang Mai, you are in Thailand's jungle, and it's here that you can make spectacular jungle treks around the city, stay overnight with local hill tribes, and learn all about their indigenous culture. These treks last from 1 day to a whole week and you'll find multiple tour agencies in Chiang Mai who offer this experience.

46. Enjoy Downtime at Erawan National Park

This 550 square kilometre park is one of the most underrated treasures in Thailand. Yes, the Thai islands are incredible, but if you really want to fall in love with Thailand's natural beauty, Erawan National Park is an absolute must-visit. There are numerous hiking trails that are suited to all kinds of fitness levels, and the number one attraction that people visit the park for is the incredible seven tier waterfall, where you can swim, bathe, and relax in the Thai sunshine.

47. Get Educated at the Lanna Folklife Museum

Considering Thailand's long and complex history, Thailand isn't a country that has a huge museum culture. Most travellers prefer to lay on the beach and eat pad thai, and that's all good, but if you want to educate yourself while in Thailand, Lanna Folklife Museum in Chiang Mai is the place. Located in a beautiful old courthouse building, on your visit here you'll learn about the old north Thai kingdom of Lanna. The dioramas of Ancient Lanna life and its religion, culture, and history, are highlights.

48. Enjoy Some Leisure Time in Lumphini Park

Bangkok is an amazing city. There are endless opportunities to eat incredible street food, party until dawn, and meet other travellers. But sometimes Bangkok can be overwhelming and there aren't too many green spaces where you can relax and enjoy some fresh air. Lumphini Park is the exception. This beautiful expanse of green has paths for trekking and hiking, an outdoor swimming pool, a beautiful lake, and plenty of Monitor Lizards roaming around.

49. Go Sea Kayaking in Krabi

In Thailand, there are tonnes of spectacular beaches, but if you're not the kind of person who wants to sit on a beach all day, there are also beach activities you can try your hand at. If you want to get adventurous at the beach, head to Krabi where there is a fun culture of watersports activities. Something that people of all fitness levels can take part in is sea kayaking. You'll have the chance to wade through the rippling clear ocean on the open waves – super cool.

50. Watch Your Jaw Drop at the Sight of The Sanctuary of Truth

Pattaya is a city in the south of Thailand that is best known for sex tourism – really not great. But beyond this, there are honestly some gems to explore in this city, and the number one has to be The Sanctuary of Truth. This temple construction is really unique because the whole thing is made from teak wood. The style is that of Khmer architecture with extraordinarily intricate wood carvings. It's more than possible to spend half a day walking around the complex, taking in the beautifully intricate work.

51. Enjoy Sunset Happy Hour on a Bangkok Rooftop Bar

Bangkok has no shortage of rooftop bars where you can experience a grand vista of the whole city, but drinks at these rooftop bars can be somewhat on the pricey side – not cool. If you head to the bar at around 5pm, however, you can find a happy hour across many of the most famous Bangkok rooftop bars. And this time is actually the best time to visit because you can experience a Bangkok sunset from a unique vantage point. The Octave Rooftop Lounge Point in Sukhumvit is one of the best spots for this.

52. Go Zip Lining in Chiang Mai

Chiang Mai is the heartland of the Thai jungle, and just outside of the city, you can enjoy an epic zip lining experience in the canopy of the jungle itself. And Chiang Mai's zip line is something out of the ordinary for true adventure enthusiasts because it's the longest zip line in all of Asia at 800 metres in length. There are fifty zip lines to choose from, so there is something for every single adventurer.

53. Enjoy the Best Fried Chicken to be Found in Bangkok

Fried chicken has to be the ultimate comfort food, but you can trust us when we say that you have not had the best fried chicken of your life until you've savoured the flavours of the chicken at Soi Polo Fried Chicken on the edge of Lumphini Park in Bangkok. This fried chicken place is known all over the city, and the best thing about it is the crispy fried garlic that is sprinkled all over your chicken. The skin is crunchy, the meat is tender – in short, it's everything that fried chicken should be.

54. Abseil Down a Waterfall in Chiang Mai

There is no shortage of stunning waterfalls in Thailand. And while they are beautiful to look at and even to take a swim in, you can up the adventure stakes by abseiling down Doi Inthanon waterfall in Chiang Mai. The height of the waterfall is around 50 metres - challenging but still doable for complete beginners. You'll feel the spray of water on you as you descend, and you'll be sure to have an enormous sense of accomplishment once you have finished your descent into the pool.

55. Get a Diving Qualification on Ko Tao

In Thailand, there are certain islands for partying, certain islands for relaxing on the beach, and others for unforgettable adventures. Ko Tao is one of the backpacker islands, but it stands out for one thing in particular, and that's its spectacular opportunities for snorkelling and diving. And, in fact, if you really want to have a holiday to remember, you can enrol in one of the diving schools on the island and actually leave with a certification to teach diving. Who knows, you might stay on the island and teach diving forever.

56. Head to Phuket for the Vegetarian Festival

When you're vegetarian and visiting Thailand, your food options can be somewhat limited. It's impossible to escape the sticks of grilled meats on every street, not to mention the fish sauce that is snuck into most Thai dishes. And so the Phuket Vegetarian Festival is a breath of fresh air. All the locals go vegetarian for ten days, so you'll be in good company. But watch out - as part of the festival, the locals also walk over hot coals, swallow swords, and pierce their bodies, all in the name of good luck. The Phuket Vegetarian Festival is typically in October of each year.

57. Chow Down on Khao Soi

When you visit Chaing Mai, there is one particular dish that you will see again and again, both on the streets and in restaurants, and that is Khao Soi. This is essentially an egg noodle curry/soup with chicken inside. The dish is very different to the tastes you will find in the south of Thailand. Instead of sharp chilli, the soup is milder, and it has a lot of turmeric and ginger inside – an influence from China and Burma.

58. Spend Active Days at Pai Canyon

Okay, Pai Canyon isn't exactly the Grand Canyon, but it is pretty darn cool regardless. Located just 8km outside of the main town of Pai itself, the landscapes are truly incredible with 360 degree panoramic views all around. You can relax and stay at the edges of the canyon, or if you are feeling active and adventurous, you can delve deep into the canyon complex and its incredible mix of rock walls and dense forest.

59. Experience Japanese Food Like a Ninja

So this one isn't exactly authentically Thai, but it's still an experience that you shouldn't skip while you're in Bangkok. Ninja House Hero is a restaurant in the trendy Sukhumvit neighbourhood that serves up tasty Japanese grub and masked ninjas provide entertainment while you eat. This isn't the cheapest dining experience in town but it's truly one of a kind and worth the splurge for the novelty factor alone.

60. Visit the Epic Mae Sa Waterfalls

One of the primary reasons that people choose to visit Chiang Mai is to take in some of the impressive surrounding waterfalls, and the coolest of them all is surely Mae Sa Waterfalls, which is only 45 minutes away from the city, but feels like you are in the deep jungle. This waterfall is simply jaw dropping, with 260 metres in height and 100 metres in width – wow! There are also lots of layers to the waterfall, which give it impressive texture for your vacation photos. Arrive early, bring a picnic, and spend the whole day splashing downstream – you will not regret it.

61. Experience a Colourful Drag Show in Bangkok

While wandering around Bangkok, you are likely to see the famous (and often very beautiful) ladyboys here and there. Gender can be something much more fluid in Thailand (and in Bangkok particularly) and drag shows are enduringly popular throughout the city. One of the slickest drag shows you'll ever see is The Calypso Show in the heart of the city, with female impersonation, dance numbers, and a healthy nod to traditional Thai culture as well.

62. Go Crazy for Lychees at the Chiang Rai Lychee Fair

Okay, unless you are really really into lychees you may not want to make a trip to Chiang Rai especially for this event, but if you happen to be in the north of Thailand, it's 100% worth making the effort. Chiang Rai is well known for its juicy and tasty lychees, and this is the ideal opportunity to enjoy a tonne of them at a rock bottom price. And just to make those lychees taste extra sweet, Chiang Rai hosts its annual beauty pageant at the same time.

63. Sip on SangSom All Night Long

When in Thailand, the usual thing to drink is beer. Singha and Chang can be found everywhere. But if you're not a beer lover, there is another option available to you: SangSom. This is marketed as Thai whisky but it's actually nothing of the sort. SangSom is a spiced rum, and it's really pretty good, having won Gold awards for liquor in both Spain and Germany. And at 40% alcohol, this is the way to start your night and to keep going into the early hours.

64. Raise Your Adrenaline With a White Water Rafting Experience

Thailand is jam packed full with beautiful beaches and stunning temples but if you want to have some experiences that raise your adrenaline, there are plenty of adventure activities in Thailand as well. For white water rafting, the best place is the Phang Nga region. There are many tour companies that can take you on an adventure across the Phraek River, promising you thrills and spills throughout every second of the journey.

65. Get Artsy at Art in Paradise in Chiang Mai

Art in Paradise in Chiang Mai is truly a one of a kind sorta place, and it's hard to say whether it's a museum, gallery, or something else altogether. Essentially, visitors are invited to peruse the halls and look at the paintings, which have been created to look as though they have a 3D effect. They can then take photos as though they are actually inside the paintings.

66. Treat Yourself to a Mud Spa

Right at the very north of Thailand in a small town called Mae Hong Son, there is a unique mud spa, the likes of which aren't often seen in Thailand. The owner offers rejuvenating treatments such as mud face masks and body wraps. There is also a café on site so once you are done, you can relax with a cup of coffee.

67. Get frisky at one of Bangkok's Gay Saunas

Okay, you'll probably only want to try this one out if you are actually gay because the term "sauna" means something a little different in the gay world. But if you are, make sure you head to Babylon in the Sathorn district. There is a beautiful outdoor pool where guys go to lounge, there is a seriously steamy steam room, and of course the standard dark rooms that you find in gay saunas. Have lots of fun and be safe!

68. Chill Out at a Hot Spring Waterfall

Visiting a waterfall is always a cool experience, and soaking your tired limbs in a hot spring is totally decadent. But what's better? A waterfall and a hot spring combined! That's exactly you will find at Namtok Ron Khlong Thom in the Krabi province. The water that tumbles down the waterfall actually originates from a hot spring, and pours down at a beautiful temperature of forty degrees celsius. Stand under the waterfall and experience a hot shower given to you by nature, and then soak into the warm water and soothe your tired limbs.

69. Indulge a Sweet Tooth With Mango & Sticky Rice

Yes, Thailand is famous for spicy snacks and noodle dishes, but the country also offers its fair share of sweet treats, and something that you can't miss (particularly if you have a sweet tooth) is mango and sticky rice. Sticky rice is cooked in sweet coconut milk and is served along freshly sliced mango. This can be found in markets, on street corners, and even in shopping malls.

70. Visit a Royal Mansion in Bangkok

One thing that you'll soon notice on your trip to Thailand is that the Royal Family is truly venerated. Cut to people becoming silent and standing to attention in a metro station at 6pm sharp. And so it's a great idea to understand more of Thailand's Royal legacy at a Royal mansion. Vimanmek Mansion located on beautifully green grounds in Bangkok is the world's largest building made totally from gold teak, and that's a good enough reason to visit. But there are also a number of things to see inside, such as the lavish interiors of a Royal mansion, and objects such as Royal carriages.

71. Take a Trip to Tao Hong Tai's Ceramics Factory

Ratchaburi is without a doubt at the centre of Thailand's ceramics culture, with over fifty ceramics factories and potters located around the area. One of the most well known is the Tao Hong Tai's Ceramics Factory, which invites tourists inside for an education on Thai pottery. Many of the pieces at Tao Hong Tai are custom made, even including pieces of ceramics furniture, and the craftsmanship on display makes a morning visit well worth the trouble.

72. Sing Your Heart Out at a Karaoke Night

There is definitely a culture of karaoke in Thailand but if you go to a local place you might not be able to keep up with all the local songs in the Thai language. Chiang Mai, however, is a city burgeoning with karaoke opportunities in English. One of the very best is a Mexican restaurant and bar called Elvis Loco. The staff are super lovely, they have a ridiculously huge selection of tracks, and they don't sell drinks by the glass but by the bucket – enough said.

73. Get Seriously Freaked Out at the Museum of Death

Yes, the Museum of Death is an actual thing, and yes, it's just about as scary as it sounds. If you enjoy the darker side of life, then this is a must visit for you while you are in Bangkok. It's officially called the Siriraj Medical Museum and contains a cross section of a human infant, a preserved foetus, children's skeletons, and all kinds of preserved medical oddities on display. Needless to say, this museum is certainly not for the faint hearted.

74. Feel Serene at the Choui Fong Tea Plantation

Not far from Chiang Rai in the north, there is one of the most celebrated tea plantations in all of Thailand, which supplies to the likes of Lipton. The vista of beautiful green tea leaves spreading for acres induces a feeling of total calm, and while you are at the plantation you can learn all about tea production, and, of course, help yourself to a cup or two while enjoying the surrounding views of Thailand's hills.

75. Experience the Drama of Bun Bangfai Rocket Festival

The start of the rainy season in May is hugely important for many Thai people because so many locals are dependent on agriculture for their income. The Bun Bangfai Rocket Festival takes place at this time as a way of encouraging rains and fertility. At the festival you can experience lots of music, dancing, parades of colourfully decorated rockets, and, of course, the launch of many a rocket as well. This festival takes place in May in the town of Yasothon.

76. Chomp on a Plateful of Quail Eggs

Okay, a fried egg might not sound terribly exotic, but once you see the cuteness of fried quail eggs along the streets of Thailand, you won't be able to resist. These are fried eggs in miniature and you are given a whole stack full on a plate, which of course you should dip into a spicy chilli sauce. The perfect protein filled pick me up to give you energy for yet more sightseeing.

77. Visit a Hindu Temple in Bangkok

When you are in Thailand, it's immediately clear that Buddhism is the prevailing religion. Bangkok is, however, a bustling city with many groups of people, and you can even find a truly stunning Hindu temple in the Silom neighbourhood. The Mariamman Temple is the number one holy place for Hindus in the city and it also happens to be a gathering place for thousands of transsexual devotees. Around the Hindu temple you can also find some awesome and cheap Indian food, so keep your eyes peeled.

78. Say Hi to the Animals in Chiang Mai Zoo

Visiting zoos is always a tricky thing for tourists who want to see animals but aren't sure how well they are looked after. Fortunately, Chiang Mai Zoo has a really good reputation for its animal welfare, which we think is super cool. Some highlights from the zoo include the panda house and their polar region. We bet you thought you'd never see a penguin in Thailand, right? Kids and adults will love this park equally.

79. Eat the Very Best Pad Thai of Your Life

When in Thailand, it's pretty much obligatory to wolf down a plate of steaming hot Pad Thai every day. But not all bowls of Pad Thai are equal, and the very best is generally considered to be made at Pad Thai Thip Samai in Bangkok. The recipe at this hole in the wall eatery begins with plump shrimps that are fried in oil, the dry noodles are then added, and other ingredients such as tofu and bean sprouts may be added per your request. It's all then wrapped in a thin omelette – delicious.

80. Get Wet and Wild at Black Mountain Water Park

Needless to say, Thailand is really really hot, and you'll want to do everything that you can to cool off during the hot and humid days – so what better than a fun trip to Thailand's best water park? At Black Mountain Water Park in Hua Hin, there is something for everyone. Thrill seekers can enjoy epic slides with sleek drops, and small kids can enjoy their own sections of the park with inflatables and lots of staff to ensure they are kept safe and secure.

81. Climb to the Top of Tonsai Tower

If you want to get your adventure on while you're in Thailand, there are few places better for an unforgettable rock climbing experience than at Tonsai Tower on Ko Phi Phi island. This 450 foot tower is certainly not for the faint hearted, but don't worry, there are plenty of tour operators with experienced instructors who can handle varying levels of expertise and make sure that everyone has a good time. And once you make it to the top, the view will make you want to scramble down and climb right back up the tower again.

82. Learn to Cook Thai Food on an Organic Farm

Everyone agrees that food is one of the best things about Thailand, so what if you weren't just eating it on the streets, but you could actually learn to make it too? You can do exactly that at many Thai cooking schools all over the country, but a particularly special one is the Thai Farm

Cooking School in Chiang Mai. You'll pick fresh ingredients straight from the farm, and learn how to cook real Thai dishes like tom yam with shrimps and yellow curry with chicken.

83. Enjoy the Chiang Mai Flower Festival

Every February in Chiang Mai, there is a festival that fills the northern city with huge amounts of colour and joy: The Chiang Mai Flower Festival. During the festival, you can look at many of the garden arrangements and floral displays, but the highlight has to be the parade of floral floats, which compete to be awarded for the most beautiful and innovative display.

84. Stroll Patpong Night Market for Your Sins

Patpong Night Market in the Silom district is world famous, or should we say infamous? Yes, this is known as one of the seediest parts of the capital, and countless people will invite you into their bars to witness a "ping pong show" but it's worth experiencing once. Not the ping pong show, the street! There is actually tonnes of stuff to buy at the market as well. It's of varying quality so use a discerning eye and be prepared to haggle hard for the right price.

85. Stay at a Floating Homestay in a Mangrove Forest

Ko Lanta is one of the most sought after islands in Thailand. It's the best place to be if you aren't quite so into the party scene and simply want to enjoy some unspoiled beauty. As well as beautiful beaches, Ko Lanta also boasts a lush mangrove forest that is well worth a visit. You can hire a kayak to explore the backwaters of the Thung Yee Pheng Mangrove Forest, but one of the best ways to experience it is by staying on the Floating House Fishfarm Homestay where you'll spot all kinds of marine life and monkeys in a luxurious atmosphere.

86. Eat Pancakes From the Street

Pancakes or rotis are a street food staple right across Thailand, and honestly, they are the perfect snack at just about any time of day, but particularly when you're leaving a nightclub and you have the late night munchies. The typical thing to eat with your pancake is sweet condensed milk and sliced bananas, but you can find all kinds of toppings such as Nutella, chocolate chips, and various jam flavours.

87. Trek Up the Golden Mountain for Some Bangkok Calm

The hustle and bustle of Bangkok is one of the very greatest things about the Thai capital, but sometimes you just want to breathe some fresh air and not have a tuk tuk driver hassling you. That's when you head for The Golden Mountain, otherwise known as Phu Khao Tong. This is an oasis right in the heart of the city, with birds flying overhead, lots of greenery and fresh air, the simple sound of temple bells ring, and even a waterfall. And once you reach the top of The Golden Mountain, you'll have a really unbelievable view across most of the city.

88. Help Out Local Animals at Lanta Animal Welfare

If you're on an extended trip in Thailand, it can be really rewarding to put the cocktails down for a second and do something to give back. While you're on the beautiful island of Ko Lanta, be sure to visit Lanta Animal Welfare, which helps sick, abused, and injured stray animals on the island. You can be taken on a guided tour to see the hard work that the staff does every day, and of course, you'll have ample opportunity to stroke and play with loving kitties and pups.

89. Clamber to the top of Wat Arun

One of the must-see temples in Bangkok is most certainly Wat Arun. On the other side of the river to Wat Pho, Wat Arun is one of few attractions on the west side of the river, and its towers are a unique fixture on the Bangkok skyline. And one of coolest features of Wat Arun is that you can climb the towers. Bear in mind that you'll need strong thighs – the climb is steep but totally worth it. And visit at around sunset for a beautiful view across the river.

90. Take a Boat Ride at Benjakiti

Anyone who has been to Bangkok will know that the city is not the greenest, but there are sprinklings of green space here and there, and Benjakiti Park is often thought of as the prettiest park in the capital. This is a place to wind down and get some fresh air, and you can also enjoy the tranquillity of its meditation, join in with a nightly yoga session, and best of all, take a romantic boat ride in a swan shaped boat on the lake. Awww.

91. Enjoy a Jungle Trek on Ko Chang

If you are the kind of traveller who enjoys jungle and forest treks, then you've probably heard that north Thailand is for you. While it's true that this region hosts many wonderful treks, don't discount some of the Thai islands. Ko Chang, in particular, has some incredibly beautiful jungle landscapes that are perfect for day treks. Many tour companies have organised treks you can join, some specialising in things like birdwatching if that takes your fancy.

92. Get Fancy at Lord Jim's Buffet

It's true that Thai street food is something really spectacular, but sometimes you want to swap your streetside plastic stool for something a little more decadent, and Lord Jim's inside the Mandarin Oriental Bangkok is exactly the place to get your eat on in an opulent environment. Their buffet lunch starts at around $45 dollars for an all you can eat seafood spread, which is huge amounts of money by Thai standards, but we promise you that it's worth everything you pay. The seafood is super fresh, you can try a selection of authentic Thai dishes, and there's even a renowned sushi bar.

93. Take a Slow Boat From Chiang Mai

If you are planning an adventure right around south-east Asia, you might be interested to know that you can take a slow boat along the Mekong River from Chiang Mai and into neighbouring Laos. Now when we say slow boat, we mean it. This trip takes three days and it can't be described as luxurious. It is, however, a wonderful way of taking down the pace a little, chilling out, enjoying the incredible views from the river, waving at local kids as they splash in the water, and to have a unique boat trip unlike any other.

94. Stay in a Treehouse on the Outskirts of Chiang Mai

To get the true Thailand experience, you have to venture away from the cities and learn what country life is all about. At Chiang Mai Tree House, you will be staying on the outskirts of Chiang Mai city, in the jungle, with only the sounds of birds tweeting and frogs croaking around you. Up in your very own teak treehouse, you will be isolated from all the stresses of everyday life, giving you the perfect opportunity to totally relax and unwind.

95. Raft Through Tham Lod Cave

If caves are your thing, you'll want to waste absolutely no time in heading to the impressive selection at Tham Lod. The whole length of the cave is around 1.5 kilometres, and in the main chamber, the cave has a height of 50 metres. There are tour companies nearby than can offer you rafting experiences through the caves. Smell the chalky smell of the walls, watch as the bats fly above your head, and be wowed by the seriously impressive stalactite formations within.

96. Walk the Longest Wooden Bridge in Thailand

Sangkhlaburi is a beautiful Thai town that sits on the border of Myanmar. Most people simply pass through when they are entering Myanmar, but it's definitely worth sticking around for a couple of days if you are in need of peace and tranquillity, if only to see the stunning handmade wooden bridge that exists there. You really do need to be careful when crossing the bridge – there are numerous holes and the repairs are a little slapdash, but that's all part of the adventure! And once you make it to the other side, there is a quaint little café where you can sip on a coffee and watch the water flow by.

97. Get a Super Cheap Wardrobe Update at Platinum Mall

Bangkok is undoubtedly a wonderful shopping city, but knowing exactly where to go is not always easy, especially if you want to shop like a local and snag yourself a fantastic deal. Cut to Platinum Fashion Mall in the centre of Bangkok. This is the place where the locals shop because it's a wholesale outlet. And wholesale shopping means wholesale prices – ker-ching! Even better – the more you buy, the more you'll be rewarded as most of the stores within the mall offer bulk discounts. You may just have to ship some items home!

98. Take a Fishing Trip on Ko Phangan

Ko Phangan may have a reputation as a party island, but in your downtime between parties, you might want to try some different activities instead of just tanning yourself on the beach. This is fishing as the locals do it – on a longtail boat and with a simple fishing rod. It's wonderfully relaxing to be out on the open sea, and your incentive for securing a big catch is that you'll be able to grill it at a beach barbecue later that evening.

99. Enrol in a Thai Language Course

One way that you are sure to impress in a foreign country and be able to boost your ability with talking to locals is by learning the foreign language. For many people travelling South America, for example, learning Spanish is a pretty standard thing to do. The Thai language, however, not so much. Yes, the sounds are more unfamiliar, and the script is different, but how rewarding would it be to learn some Thai basics? There are language schools all around the country that can help you out with this, but A.U.A language school in Chiang Mai is one with a great reputation.

100. Party With Young Thai People at Route 66

When you are a tourist in a foreign country, you are bound to do some touristic things. That is totally cool, but it can also be great to do something that locals would do aside from the major sights and attractions. If you love to party and want to hit the dancefloor with local young Thai people, forget the backpacker heavy Khao San Road and head to Route 66 Club in Bangkok. There are different rooms for different kinds of music lovers, but if you really want to get down with the locals, try the Thai Pop room.

101. Visit the World's Largest Crocodile Farm

With more than 60,000 crocodiles on the premises, the Samut Prakan Crocodile Farm just outside of Bangkok is undoubtedly the place to be if you want to see a croc. If you want to get there for feeding time, 4:30pm every day is when you need to be at the farm, and you'll also be able to catch the staff wrestling with the crocodiles.

Before You Go...

Hey you! Thanks so much for reading **101 Coolest Things to Do in Thailand**. We really hope that this helps to make your time in Thailand the most fun and memorable trip that it can be. And if you enjoyed reading the book, it would be super cool if you could leave a review on the book's Amazon web page. Thank you!

Keep your eyes peeled on www.101coolestthings.com and have a wonderful trip.

The 101 Coolest Things Team

Made in the USA
San Bernardino, CA
12 December 2016